D0516121

Pachycephalosaurus

by Daniel Cohen

Consultant:
Larry Dean Martin, Ph.D.
Professor-Senior Curator
Natural History Museum and Biodiversity Research Center
University of Kansas, Lawrence, Kansas

Bridgestone Books
an imprint of Capstone Press
Mankato, Minnesota

Bridgestone Books are published by Capstone Press
151 Good Counsel Drive, P.O. Box 669, Mankato, Minnesota 56002
http://www.capstonepress.com

Library of Congress Cataloging-in-Publication Data
Cohen, Daniel, 1936-
    Pachycephalosaurus / by Daniel Cohen.
    p. cm.—(Discovering dinosaurs)
    Summary: Describes what is known about the physical characteristics, behavior, and habitat
of this bony-headed, plant-eating dinosaur.
    Includes bibliographical references and index.
    ISBN 0-7368-2523-1 (hardcover)
    1. Pachycephalosaurus—Juvenile literature. [1. Pachycephalosaurus. 2. Dinosaurs.] I. Title.
QE862.O65C622 2004
567.914—dc21   2003010805

Editorial Credits
Amanda Doering, editor; Linda Clavel, series designer; Enoch Peterson, cover production
    designer and illustrator; Alta Schaffer, photo researcher; Karen Risch, product planning
    editor

Photo Credits
Capstone Press/Scott Thoms, 16
Corbis/Richard T. Nowitz, 14
Francois Gohier, 18
The Natural History Museum/J. Sibbick, 6; Orbis, 4, 8, 12
Triebold Paleontology Inc., cover, 1, 10

1 2 3 4 5 6 09 08 07 06 05 04

Table of Contents

Pachycephalosaurus compared to a
5-foot-tall (1.5-meter-tall) human

Pachycephalosaurus

Pachycephalosaurus was a **dinosaur** that ate plants. Pachycephalosaurus (pak-ee-SEF-ah-lo-sore-us) means "thick-headed reptile." This dinosaur measured 13 to 26 feet (4 to 8 meters) long. It weighed 1 to 2 tons (0.9 to 1.8 metric tons).

6

The World of Pachycephalosaurus

Pachycephalosaurus lived in what is now western North America. It lived there 75 million years ago. Earth was different during the time pachycephalosaurus lived. The climate was warmer and wetter than it is today.

climate
the usual weather in a place

Stegoceras

Relatives of Pachycephalosaurus

Pachycephalosaurus was a part of a small group of dinosaurs called pachycephalosaurs. These dinosaurs were also called "bone-headed dinosaurs." Stegoceras (ste-GOS-er-as) was a relative of pachycephalosaurus.

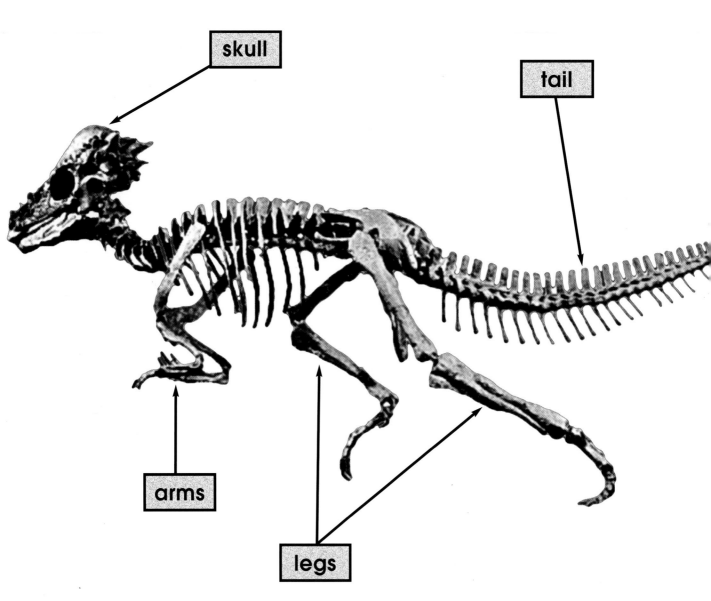

skull

tail

arms

legs

Parts of Pachycephalosaurus

Pachycephalosaurus walked upright on its large hind legs. Its arms were small. Pachycephalosaurus used its thick tail for **balance**. It had a thick domed skull. Pachycephalosaurus' skull was up to 10 inches (25 centimeters) thick. Knobs and spines stuck out of its skull.

spine
a hard, sharp, pointed growth

Thick-Skulled Dinosaur

Scientists once thought that two pachycephalosaurs would butt heads to fight. But pachycephalosaurus' skull and neck were not strong enough to fight this way. Pachycephalosaurus might have used its head to hit other dinosaurs in softer areas.

Albertosaurus

Predators

Large, meat-eating predators like albertosaurus (al-BERT-oh-sore-us) could have hunted pachycephalosaurus. Pachycephalosaurus could chase away smaller meat-eaters. It may have charged smaller dinosaurs with its thick, spiked skull.

predator
an animal that hunts and eats other animals

What Pachycephalosaurus Ate

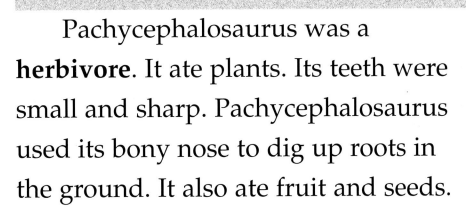

Pachycephalosaurus was a **herbivore**. It ate plants. Its teeth were small and sharp. Pachycephalosaurus used its bony nose to dig up roots in the ground. It also ate fruit and seeds.

End of Pachycephalosaurus

Pachycephalosaurus lived at the end of the dinosaur age 65 million years ago. All of the dinosaurs that lived at this time became **extinct**. Some scientists think that a giant meteorite from space hit Earth. The effects from the meteorite caused the dinosaurs to die.

meteorite
a rock from space that strikes Earth

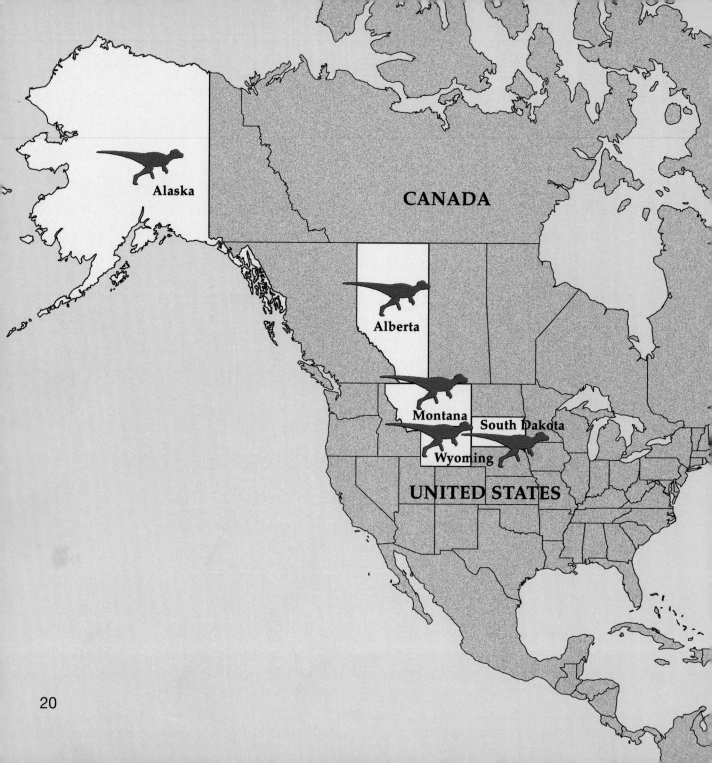

Alaska

CANADA

Alberta

Montana

South Dakota

Wyoming

UNITED STATES

Discovering Pachycephalosaurus

Pachycephalosaurus was discovered in Montana in 1938. Other **fossils** were found in western North America. Complete skeletons of pachycephalosaurus are rare. Usually, just a thick skull fossil is found.

Hands On: Thick and Thin Treasure Hunt

A pachycephalosaurus skull was up to 10 inches (25 centimeters) thick. A person's skull is only .25 inch (0.6 centimeter) thick. Go on an indoor or outdoor treasure hunt to find things that are the same thickness as your skull or a pachycephalosaurus skull.

What You Need

notebook
pencil
ruler or tape measure

What You Do

1. On one notebook page, write 10 inches (25 centimeters) at the top. On another page, write 0.25 inches (0.6 centimeter). This is where you will keep track of the objects you find.
2. Look around the room or outside for things that might be as thick as a pachycephalosaurus skull. Then find things as thin as your skull. Measure those things with the ruler or tape measure to make sure.
3. On the correct notebook page, write down the objects. Record where you found the object in case you want to find it again. Find at least five things for each page.
4. Compare the two lists and objects. How many of the 0.25-inch (0.6-centimeter) objects would it take to equal the thickness of one 10-inch (25-centimeter) object?

Glossary

balance (BAL-uhnss)—ability to keep steady without falling

dinosaur (DYE-na-sore)—an extinct land reptile; dinosaurs lived on Earth at least 150 million years.

extinct (ek-STINGKT)—no longer living anywhere in the world

fossil (FOSS-uhl)—the remains or traces of something that once lived; bones and footprints can be fossils.

herbivore (HUR-buh-vor)—an animal that eats only plants

scientist (SYE-uhn-tist)—a person who studies the world around us

Read More

Holmes, Thom, and Laurie Holmes. *Armored, Plated, and Bone-Headed Dinosaurs: The Ankylosaurs, Stegosaurs, and Pachycephalosaurs.* The Dinosaur Library. Berkeley Heights, N.J.: Enslow, 2002.

Schomp, Virginia. *Pachycephalosaurus and Other Bone-Headed Plant-Eaters.* Prehistoric World. New York: Benchmark Books, 2004.

Internet Sites

FactHound offers a safe, fun way to find Internet sites related to this book. All of the sites on FactHound have been researched by our staff.

Here's how:
1. Visit *www.facthound.com*
2. Type in this special code **0736825231** for age-appropriate sites. Or enter a search word related to this book for a more general search.
3. Click on the Fetch It button.

FactHound will fetch the best sites for you!

Index

1074540541